P9-DCW-517

GRASSLANDS

A TRUE BOOK

by
Darlene R. Stille

Children's Press®
A Division of Grolier Publishing

New York London Hong Kong Sydney
Danbury, Connecticut

A grassland in Africa

Reading Consultant
Linda Cornwell
*Coordinator of School Quality
and Professional Improvement
Indiana State Teachers
Association*

Content Consultant
Jan Jenner, Ph.D.

Author's Dedication
*For Cynthia A. Marquard,
who showed me some of the
world's great ecosystems.*

**Visit Children's Press® on the
Internet at:
http://publishing.grolier.com**

*The photo on the cover shows
a prairie in Lawrence County,
Missouri. The photo on the
title page shows a steppe
in Wyoming.*

Library of Congress Cataloging-in-Publication Data

Stille, Darlene R.
    Grasslands / by Darlene R. Stille.
        p.   cm. — (A true book)
    Includes bibliographical references and index.
    Summary: Examines the different types of grasslands and the plant and
animal life they support.
    ISBN: 0-516-21509-4 (lib. bdg.)   0-516-26762-0 (pbk.)
    1. Grasslands—Juvenile literature. [1. Grasslands.]   I. Title. II. Series
QH87.7.S75 1999
578.74—dc21   98-49728
                                                                                   CIP
                                                                                   AC

Contents

Grass grows in
most playgrounds.

Grass and Grasslands

Everyone has seen grass. It grows in most parks and playgrounds. It also grows around most houses.

There are many different kinds of grass in the world. Cows and horses eat one kind of grass. People eat grasses too. Did you know

Wheat is a type of grass (left). Wheat seeds are ground and made into flour for bread and other foods (above).

that wheat, corn, rice, barley, rye, and oats are all types of grass?

Very large, flat areas of land covered with grass are called grasslands. Grasslands are found in many parts of the world.

Prairies

Prairies are grasslands that have patches of wildflowers and a few scattered trees. There are many different kinds of prairie grasses. Big bluestem, little bluestem, Indian grass, switch grass, and blue grama are the names of a few prairie grasses.

This prairie near Leona, South Dakota, has long grasses and a variety of wildflowers.

Some of these grasses can grow as tall as an adult.

9

The beautiful wildflowers that grow on prairies come in many different colors. Goldenrods, coneflowers, and sunflowers are yellow. Blazing stars and asters are purple.

Prairie roses are pink. The trees on prairies grow near streams and rivers.

Prairies have hot summers and cold, snowy winters. In spring and fall, prairies get a lot of rain.

In winter, many prairies are covered with snow.

Steppes

Steppes (STEPS) are grasslands with short wild grasses,
such as blue grama, buffalo
grass, wheat grass, and spear
grass. Steppe grasses are
usually less than 12 inches (30
centimeters) tall. Like prairies,
steppes have hot summers
and cold winters. But steppes

Steppes are much drier than prairies.

get less rain. As a result,
the grass on steppes is not
as thick as prairie grass.

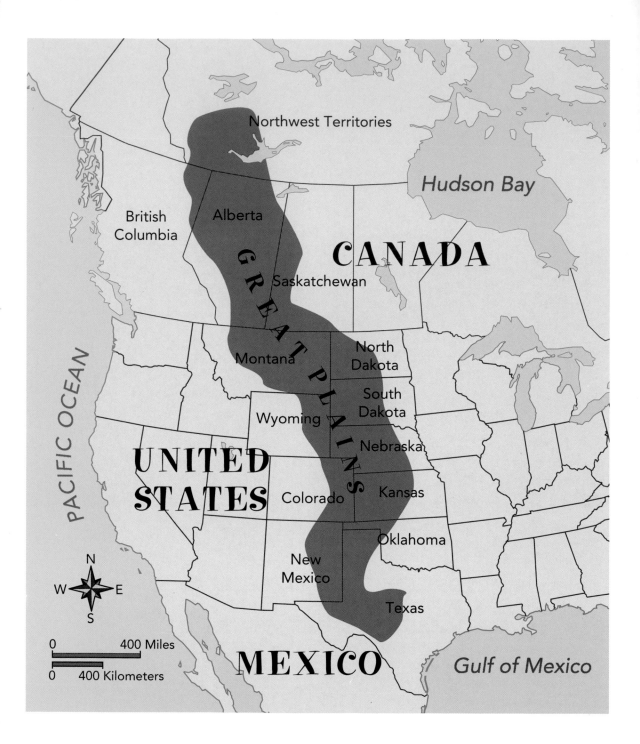

One the most famous steppes in the world is the Great Plains of North America. This steppe includes most of the central United States and Canada. It stretches from the Northwest Territories of Canada to the states of Texas and New Mexico. There is also a huge steppe in southern Russia and central Asia. Many smaller steppes are found in other parts of the world.

The Dust

When no rain falls on steppes, the soil dries out. Then, strong winds can blow the loose soil away. When steppes are turned into farmland, the soil can blow away very easily.

In the 1930s, there was almost no rain for seven years in parts of Oklahoma, Kansas, Texas, and New Mexico. When strong winds blew, dust from loose soil piled up around houses like snowdrifts. The dust in

Bowl

the air was so thick that some people even got lost during these dust storms. Around that time, many people started calling this area of the United States "the Dust Bowl."

In the 1930s, many farms in the Dust Bowl were destroyed.

Prairie and Steppe Animals

Many of the animals that live on prairies are found on steppes, too. Rabbits, deer, antelope, mice, squirrels, and prairie dogs all eat the grasses. These mammals are hunted by foxes, coyotes, and badgers as well as lizards and rattlesnakes.

A herd of pronghorn antelope (above) and a black-tailed prairie dog (right)

A red fox (left) and a prairie rattlesnake (below)

Hundreds of kinds of birds live on prairies and steppes. Blackbirds, grouse, meadow-larks, quail, and other birds build their nests in the thick grasses. These birds feed on

A meadowlark (above) and a grasshopper (right)

the grasshoppers, ants, beetles, and other insects that crawl on the grasses. Some also eat the insects that burrow in the soil. Hawks and owls prey on small mammals.

This bison lives in Yellowstone National Park, where it is safe from hunters.

One of the most famous animals of the American prairies and steppes is the bison, or buffalo. At one time, millions of bison roamed the Great Plains of North America. In the late 1800s, white hunters killed so many bison that these animals almost became extinct. Now some bison live in protected areas, such as national parks. Others live on ranches.

Fire

Fires are a natural part of the circle of life on grasslands.

and Grasslands

You probably think of fires as bad, but wild grasslands need fire. Natural fires are caused by lightning. They burn until rain puts them out or until the flames reach a river. Fire burns the part of grass above the ground, but it does not harm the roots. When fire destroys grasses, the ashes make the soil richer. Soon new grass grows in the burned area. People who want to restore natural grasses sometimes set a grassland on fire.

Savannas

Savannas are large, flat grass-lands with clumps of trees and shrubs. They are found in parts of Africa, Australia, India, and South America.

Savannas are hot all year long. They do not have four seasons like prairies and steppes. Instead, they have

A savanna in the African country of Kenya

A savanna in
Queensland, Australia

one rainy season and one dry season. Some savannas get more rain than others. The type of plants that grow on a savanna depends on how much rain falls there.

On dry savannas, the grass is only a few inches tall and there are just a few trees. On wet savannas, the grass can be 10 feet (3 meters) high. That's almost twice as tall as most adults! More rain means more trees. Acacias,

This baobab tree has leaves during the wet season.

baobabs, and snappy gums are some of the trees that grow on savannas.

Animals of the Savanna

Antelope, zebras, cheetahs, and lions all live on savannas. Antelope and zebras live in herds. They eat the grasses and small shrubs that grow on African savannas.

Cheetahs, lions, and other meat-eating animals feed on

Herds of zebras live on savannas in East Africa (above). They have many enemies, including the cheetah (right).

antelope and zebras. Small mammals, birds, and reptiles eat the insects that live on savannas.

Many people travel to the African savannas to see the amazing animals that live there. Trips to see savanna animals

Most people visiting the African savannas hope to see a lion.

A group of tourists take pictures of elephants at Masai Mara National Reserve in Kenya.

are called safaris. In the past, people went on safaris to shoot lions and other large animals. Now they only are allowed to take pictures.

Saving Grasslands

Early pioneers who crossed the American West saw one of the biggest steppes in the world. Some settlers said that when the tall grasses blew in the wind, they looked like the waves on an ocean. To cross this sea of grass, they used wagons

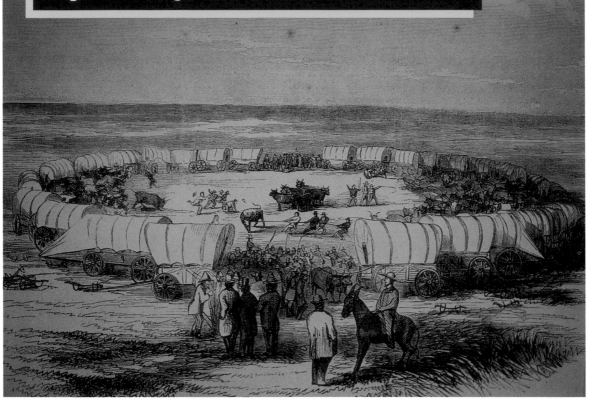

called "prairie schooners."
A schooner is a kind of
boat.

That huge steppe no longer exists. Large parts of it have been plowed under to create farmland or to make room for

Today North American wheat fields cover land that was once part of a huge steppe.

buildings. Today wheat fields and shopping malls have replaced the wild grasses.

Most of the large prairies and steppes that once grew in other parts of the world are also long gone. At one time, grasslands spread across Argentina, South Africa, New Zealand, and eastern Europe.

Luckily, a few grasslands are left. The Badlands National Grassland in South

You can still see large areas of wild grassland in Badlands National Grassland in South Dakota.

Giraffes are just one of the many animals that live on Africa's protected savannas.

Dakota is one example. If you visit this part, you will get an idea of what the Great Plains looked like two hundred years ago. Some savannas still exist in Africa. These grasslands—and the animals that live on them—are protected by law.

Many people want to protect the grasslands that still exist. This can be done if ranchers don't let their animals eat too much grass in

These volunteers are planting grass seed. They hope that this area can be restored to a grassland.

one area. Other people hope to plant the seeds of wild grasses in areas that were once covered by grasslands. Then they plan to leave the land alone, so it will become wild grassland again.

To Find Out More

Here are some additional resources to help you learn more about grasslands:

Books

Bauer, Erwin A. and Peggy Bauer. **Save Our Prairies and Grasslands.** Delacorte Press, 1994.

Burr, Deborah (illus.). **Animals of the Grasslands.** Flying Frog Publishing, 1997.

Houle, Mary. **The Prairie Keepers: Secrets of the Grasslands.** Raintree Steck-Vaughn Publishers, 1997.

Lambert, David. **People of the Grasslands.** Raintree Steck-Vaughn Publishers, 1998.

Pipes, Rose. **Grasslands.** Raintree Steck-Vaughn Publishers, 1998.

Radley, Gail. **Grasslands and Deserts.** Lerner Publishing Group, 1998.

Savage, Stephen. **Animals of the Grasslands.** Raintree Steck-Vaughn Publishers, 1997.

Organizations and Online Sites

Chase Lake Prairie Project

http://www.r6.fws.gov/ REFUGES/chase/clpp.htm

This site describes how the National Forest Service is trying to restore prairie land in North Dakota.

Meadowbrook Prairie

http://www.prairienet.org/ meadowbrook/

Enjoy a story and pictures about a prairie near Urbana, Illinois.

Northern Prairie Biological Resources

http://www.npwrc.usgs.gov /resource/resource.htm

This site features pictures of many prairie plants and animals.

Pawnee National Grassland

http://www.fs.fed.us/arnf/ png/

The National Forest Service provides information for visiting a grassland area in Colorado.

Shortgrass Steppe Long-term Ecological Research

http://sgs.cnr.colostate.edu

Find out more about plants and animals that live in steppe areas.

Important Words

extinct no longer existing

prairie a grassland that receives plenty of rain, often has tall grasses, patches of wildflowers, and few trees

savanna flat grassland with clumps of trees and shrubs

schooner a type of boat

soil the dirt and other materials that make up the top layer of earth

steppe a grassland that receives very little rainfall, usually has short wild grasses and few trees

46

Index

(**Boldface** page numbers indicate illustrations.)

Meet the Author

Darlene R. Stille lives in Chicago, Illinois, and is executive editor of the World Book Annuals and World Book's Online Service. She has written many books for Children's Press, including *Extraordinary Women Scientists*, *Extraordinary Women of Medicine*, four True Books about the human body, and four other True Books about ecosystems.